[ZHINGOORA BOOKS]

This digital edition is published by
Zhingoora Books.

The Cover is Designed by Pallav Sethiya.

Apart from any fair dealing for the purposes
of research or private study, or criti-cism or
review, as permitted under the Copyright,
Designs and Patents Act 1988, this
publication may only be reproduced, stored
or transmitted, in any form or by any means,
with the prior permission in writing of the
publishers. All disputes are subject to
exclusive jurisdiction of Mandsaur Courts
only. For any suggestions and feedback or
book on new concept/domain, please contact
us at the email given below.

zhingoora_books@yahoo.com

CONTENTS

A THANKSGIVING SURPRISE.

SLEIGHING SONG.

Hurrah! Hurrah! for the jolly snow!Over it we lightly go:Dear sister is so glad, you see,To have a nice drive in the sleigh with me,To have a nice drive in the sleigh with me—Hurrah! Hurrah! Hurrah!

Hurrah! Hurrah for the ice and cold!Both very young and gay and bold,We fear no snow, we fear no ice,There's naught in the world that is half so nice,There's naught in the world that is half so nice—Hurrah! Hurrah! Hurrah!

FOOD FOR HER LITTLE ONES

Over the lofty peaks of many of the mountains of Europe a magnificent bird may occasionally be seen flying, while down in the valley, two thousand feet or more below, a hen may be scratching worms for her dinner, or a young lamb gamboling over the sweet meadow grass.

From that enormous height, even, the keen eyes of the eagle can detect the movement of either, and she flies, or rather drops, straight down upon the poor fowl, and with her powerful foot kills it at a blow, or breaks the back of the pretty lamb with same terrible weapon. Then, she rises upward with her prey, to feed the little ones she has left in the nest.

A BUSY STREET

Here you have a picture of busy street-life in a great city. Everybody is in a hurry and everybody wishes to get ahead. The man at the left has loaded his wagon so high that he finds it hard to hold the reins. Do you see the cunning little dog in the pony-cart? He means to see all there is about him.

A BUSY STREET

THE NEW DOLL'S CARRIAGE

At Christmas Jessie had a pretty French doll given to her by her aunt Amy. For weeks Jessie thought she had nothing more to wish for, but in the spring, however, when the days were warm and sunny, and nature called her out-of-doors, she found it rather inconvenient to take her dolly with her every time. She couldn't use her arms for anything else, you see, and like every other child, she liked to run and jump, and pick flowers and other things that caught her eye. But, like a good little mother, she thought her dolly needed the fresh air quite as much as herself; so one night, at the supper-table, she said: "I wish I had a carriage for Bella, then I could leave her in that when I went for buttercups and violets."

Papa was present, and he heard her remark. In a few days Jessie's birthday would come, and both he and her mamma had been thinking of what they would give her then; for Jessie was such a good, gentle child, seldom teasing for what she could not have, that they always took especial care to remember her on such holidays.

The innocent hint was just what he wanted. So on the birthday morn, Jessie found Bella seated in a beautiful little carriage, close beside her chair at the breakfast-table. You may be sure she was a very happy little girl then, and that she gave mamma and papa many loving hugs and kisses for their thoughtfulness and love.

JOSIE'S FRIEND.

A TRUE STORY.

I must tell you what happened to my little girl, for we all thought it so wonderful.

She was a dear child, only seven years old, and so anxious to have a friend all her own. One day I took her to Boston. She was wild with joy at being allowed to take such a long trip in the cars. As the train steamed out from Newport, Josie's happy little face was pressed close to the window; but after a while she grew less interested in the fields outside, and more so in the passengers near us.

"O mamma!" she whispered to me, "do you see that little girl opposite? I want her for a friend so much!"

[10]

The child she had noticed was indeed a sweet little girl, with hair almost as golden as Josie's own. She was soon smiling at Josie, and the two little travellers held up their dollies for each other to look at.

But before we got to Boston my little girl had grown weary, and soon was fast asleep. When we reached Boston she awoke, and saw her little friend disappearing. Josie waved her hand to her, and then, to my great surprise, shut her eyes tight.

"Why, darling," I said, "didn't you hear mamma tell you this was Boston? Don't go to sleep again; there are auntie and little Bess."

"Mamma," she answered gravely, "I was not going to sleep. I was asking God to let that little girl be my friend."

"But, my dear," I said, "you live in Newport, and you have only seen her in the cars. She probably lives in Boston. Come, auntie is hunting for us."

Josie had a fine time at auntie's, and her cousin Bess for a while filled completely the position of friend. But the week over, and we were aboard the train for Newport; and Josie's mind was again filled with the all-engrossing subject of—a friend.

We arrived at home in time for luncheon. Immediately after, Josie was in her room telling her sister all about her visit. Suddenly I heard a cry of joy. "O mamma! mamma! There she is! God did send her."

I hurried into Josie's room, and there at the window stood Josie, holding up her doll, and smiling at the window of the next house.

A second glance showed me that this was the very child we had seen in the cars.

The little girls soon became acquainted, for little Carrie had come to spend the winter with the Endicotts, who owned the house next our cottage.

No words can tell how happy my Josie has been with the little friend God sent her.

BUTTERFLY WISDOM.

A butterfly poised on a wild-rose spray,As a child tripped by one summer day,And he thought: "How sorrowful she must beTo know she can never have wings like me!"But the child passed on, with a careless eyeOf the gay-winged, proud, young butterfly,While he fluttered about, as butterflies will,Sipping of honey and dew his fill.

The butterfly spread his wings to the sky,As the sweet-faced child again tripped by,And he thought: "How envious she will beMy beautiful azure wings to see!"But the child passed, with a lightsome heart,Where never had lodged a poisonous dart,While he fluttered about, as butterflies will,Sipping of honey and dew his fill.

When the child again passed the wild-rose sweet,A bit of azure fell at her feet;She lifted it from the moss, and said:—"Poor little butterfly, it is dead!"Then she tossed it up towards the wild-rose spray,And, singing merrily, went her way,With never a thought, the summer through,Of the butterfly and its wings of blue.

MR. MONKEY.

Oh, fun, fun, fun! Is there anything half so funny in this world as a monkey?

Just listen a moment, and I will tell you of one that I saw the other day.

Think what a proud monkey he must have been, dressed in a fine suit of clothes! Then to have every one look out of the window when he rung the bell, while he sat up on the corner of the hand-organ. And how the children laughed to see him! After he had called every one within hearing to look at him, he made a little bow and took off his hat very politely.

Then he put down the bell, and his master gave him cymbals, which he banged together in a lively way.

How delighted all were to see that Mr. Monkey was a student! It was so very queer to see the little scholar wearing those spectacles which the hand-organ man put on his nose; how well he held the tiny book, no matter if it was wrong side up!

Mr. Monkey would have made a good farmer, we all said, when we saw him churn. The way that handle flew up and down would have made milk into butter very shortly, if there had been milk there.

Next came the fiddle, a nice little one, just the right size for a monkey to play. The hand-organ sounded very slowly while the little monkey played his fiddle. For fear that his master would feel badly because he was so far behind, Mr. Monkey put away his instrument, and bowed very low to the people, taking off his hat to thank them for the many pennies showered upon him.

A Ride·in·A Water·Wheel·

A TRUE STORY.

Bertie Gale lived near a noisy little brook, which went singing through the meadow. Just below the house in which he lived was a dam. It made a large pond above it, and the water was used to turn the wheel of a small woollen-mill.

It was such fun to watch the water pouring over the wheel, turning it swiftly round and round.

Bertie was never tired of looking at it, but it made his mother very anxious if her little boy was long out of her sight. But he had promised never to go into the water without permission.

But one summer the water was shut off for a while, and the mill was silent. The old wheel was badly decayed and broken, and Mr. Gale said a new wheel must be built.

Every day Bertie hurried home from school to watch his father and the workmen, as they built the new wheel.

One day when he came home, he ran down to the mill as usual. The wheel was in its place all ready for action.

How new and clean it looked! The workmen had gone, and no one was in sight.

"What a nice playhouse it would make," thought the boy. Then he stepped carefully into the wheel.

"This is my castle," said Bertie to himself, "and the brook is the river Rhine, and"—

Bertie did not finish his sentence. Suddenly there was a terrible roaring over his head, and the wheel began to go slowly around. The next thing the boy knew he was lying upon a pile of blocks and shavings, feeling very much as if he had been through his mother's sausage-mill, but very thankful that he was not still going around that swiftly-moving wheel. He was not very much hurt, but it was a long time before he cared to look at the water-wheel again.

JAMIE.

One day lit-tle Jam-ie went with some friends to see some mov-ing pic-tures and a play called "The Johns-town Flood." He had been told the sto-ry be-fore and knew how it turned out. So he sat ver-y still through three acts, and then he saw a man who had been giv-en the name of "Paul Re-vere" just for that play, be-cause he was go-ing to do some-thing such as a real and great Paul Revere once did, more than a hun-dred years be-fore, a thing to warn the land of dan-ger and help the peo-ple to be free.

The man in the play had to mount a horse and gal-lop down a val-ley shout-ing to the peo-ple to go to the hills to get out of the way of a great flood which had bro-ken out from a res-er-voir a-bove the cit-y.

[23]

Just then, as the man mount-ed the horse, on the stage, little Jam-ie left his seat and ran home as fast as he could.

"Why, Jam-ie," said his moth-er "The show can't be o-ver yet, it's on-ly four o'clock."

"I know it is-n't o-ver yet, mam-ma," said Jam-ie, "but the ver-y next act was to be the flood, and I thought that if I staid I'd be drowned!"

MOTHER'S CHILDREN

"El-sie, just mind the ba-by for a few min-utes while I fin-ish Jack's lit-tle trou-sers. He tears his clothes so that it's just patch, patch, put in pockets and sew on but-tons all the time."

"Oh, moth-er, look! Ba-by has tak-en a step! Come quick and look at him!"

So moth-er ran to see her ba-by-boy, and kiss the brave lit-tle fel-low who had dared to do this won-der-ful thing. She a-gain seat-ed her-self at her work, when she heard El-sie call, "Oh, mam-ma! Sa-die has got hold of grand-ma's bas-ket, and is toss-ing all the things out of it on the floor. She'll scream when I take it from her, but don't wor-ry, I think I can man-age her."

It was not long aft-er that when mam-ma cried out, "Why, there must be some-thing burn-ing! Oh, where is Tom-my? He has so many tricks with fire!"

Up jumped mam-ma a-gain, and run-ing in-to the li-bra-ry, found Tom-my in high glee at play in front of a bright coal fire in the grate, on the top bar of which was a row of small fig-ures made from dough that cook was work-ing in the kitch-en. Tom had seized a big piece of dough, ran off with it to the li-bra-ry, and mould-ed it up to suit him in the shape of a row of small boys tak-ing hold of hands. He set them on the hot i-ron bar, and was brown-ing them ready to eat!

"This is great fun, moth-er!" said Tom. "I'll give the chil-dren some when they are baked!"

VICTOR.

"It's a nice thing to have spring come!" said Vic-tor.

"With my red wheel-barrow I can work out in the gar-den ev-er-y day with O-bed. He says he'd rath-er have me with him than an-y two men! Why, I can car-ry a wa-ter-ing-pot, a lot of twigs, leaves and things I've raked off the flow-er beds, and some-times I e-ven car-ry a whole load of stones!

"O-bed is go-ing to teach me how to make one gar-den-bed for my-self. He says I can plant an-y-thing there that I like. I'm try-ing to think what I do like. O-bed says that some things come up when you plant seeds and some come up from bulbs. I like po-ta-toes and sweet peas. I guess I'll plant them. For a bor-der, I'd like small on-ions. Seems to me some tur-nips and hol-ly-hocks would look well in my bed. Now would-n't they? Sweet corn grows up pret-ty and grace-ful, I heard Aunt Hat-tie say, so I'll have some of that in my bed with a lot of for-get-me-nots. Aun-tie likes those ver-y much.

"Oh, I must have the fa-vor-ite flow-ers of each one in our house, come to think of it! Let's see, what is Papa's fa-vor-ite flow-er? I guess it must be squash, for he likes mam-ma's squash pies so much.

"Now what is mam-ma's? It must be he-li-o-trope. It's a hard word, but I've sure-ly heard her say he-li-o-trope sach-et. It must be a pret-ty flower, for ev-er-y thing in the clothes press has that per-fume, Ka-tie says.

"Now I don't know all these plants I've heard folks talk about. I don't know an-y of them. Per-haps be-fore I tell O-bed to get all these things for me to start I'd bet-ter ask him if they'll go well to-geth-er."

GRANDMOTHER'S HOME.

Grand-moth-er Gra-ham was a love-ly old la-dy. She had a beau-ti-ful home a few miles from the city. Her chil-dren and her grand-chil-dren went out to see her quite oft-en.

A-my thought there was no place like Grand-ma's for her sum-mer va-ca-tion. There was a lake, a boat, white lil-ies, squir-rels, grand trees old-er than grand-moth-er, her-self. Then there were barns, sta-bles, hor-ses, cows, calves, and a Shet-land pony that an-y child could ride.

A-my had her bi-cy-cle with her, and went off on it to see Grand-ma's neigh-bors and do any lit-tle er-rands that were re-quired. If cous-in Jam-ie were on a vis-it at the same time, per-haps he would

mount Gyp-sy, the po-ny, and ride a-long by Am-y's side. A race be-
tween the bi-cy-cle and the po-ny was great fun.

But there were days when rains kept the chil-dren in the house.
Grand-ma told them love-ly sto-ries then. Jam-ie would sit play-ing
with his sol-diers, and A-my al-ways had all she could do in her
"house-days" as she called them, sew-ing to "keep her dolls in
clothes," for "Elm Lodge" was a great place to wear out clothes.

The sto-ries Grand-ma liked best to tell were "true sto-ries" of the
days when her own chil-dren were small, and A-my liked best to
hear a-bout her own fa-ther and what he did when he was a child.
So one day grand-ma told this:

GRANDMOTHER'S STORY.

"My lit-tle Har-vey was ver-y fond of fruit and flow-ers. When he was a wee bit of a lad he liked noth-ing bet-ter than to pull the tu-lips off by their heads and fill the crown of his hat with them. We told him that he must not do this, for there were not e-nough of them to waste in that way. He looked sad, but sat down un-der a tree, and seemed in deep thought. He was-n't more than three years old then.

"We left him and went in-to the house. In a few min-utes he went soft-ly down the gar-den walk, took off his shoes, stooped down, and scooped up earth e-nough to fill them, and then, in his stock-ing-feet, ran in a-mong the tulips and filled each cup full of the earth, emp-ty-ing all from his shoes in-to them. Daugh-ter and I had been watch-ing the child from the li-bra-ry win-dow. We crept out of the house and got in-to the gar-den as quick-ly as we could, and peep-ing be-hind the hon-ey suc-kle ar-bor, lis-tened while the lit-tle fel-low talked a-loud. 'Now 'ou tu-lips, dear, make haste and grow. All this dirt will make 'ou grow, I know, and then there'll be e-nough tu-lips for me to fill my 'it-tle hat full ev'ry day!'

"The lis-ten-ers had to laugh at that. My ba-by-boy dropped his shoes and ran as fast as he could a-way from us, 'round-and-'round, through the damp gar-den paths! He led us quite a chase be-fore we could catch him."

How A-my and Jam-ie laughed when Grand-ma told "tales out of school" as she called them.

ALL HER CHILDREN LIKED TO VISIT GRANDMA.

"But I must just tell you this, my dear, for the tu-lip-story al-ways makes me think of it.

"There came a day, at last, when we had to send Har-vey to school. Tom-my Short took him, with his green wool-len bag, slate, pen-cil, and two cook-ies, just round the cor-ner to Miss Burt's school. After a few weeks, Grand-pa Chase met the new pu-pil in the gar-den one day, just as he came in from school.

"'Well, Har-vey' said Grandpa, 'I suppose you can spell al-most an-y thing by this time!'

"'Yes, sir?' said Har-vey.

"'Can you spell rat?'

"'R-a-t, rat' said the small boy, with much pride.

"'Ver-y well, my boy. Now can you spell mouse?'

"Har-vey wrink-led up his fore-head and tried hard to think how it could be done. Aft-er a few min-utes the child said, 'No, Grandpa, I can't do it.'

"'What,' cried Grandpa Chase, 'you can spell a great rat and can't spell a lit-tle bit of a mouse!'

"A-gain Har-vey thought hard, and then he said, 'Yes I can spell a big rat, but I guess a spelt mouse is a great deal big-ger than a spelt rat!'"

CHEER UP!

You do not like this weath-er, Ralph,But March is pass-ing by,We'll sure-ly have bright days at last,With A-pril's laugh-ing sky.

CHILDREN'S WORK.

The Berk-ville Ham-let School pu-pils took much in-ter-est in the Fresh Air Chil-dren who had been sent out to their vil-lage for sum-mer out-ings. They had thought of ways in which mon-ey could be raised to help a-long the good cause.

"Why could-n't we have some tab-leaux and oth-er things in our school house on Sa-tur-day af-ter-noons in May?" asked Jen-nie Hill. "Tom-my Burns would print the tickets and all the chil-dren in the vil-lage will, I know, sell them."

So the mat-ter was talked ov-er, and all the peo-ple liked the plan so much that the young folks soon be-gan to prac-tice their parts for the first day.

Le-on and Ef-fie King were to wear old time cos-tumes, stand ver-y still, and not speak. They made a pleas-ing tab-leau. There was a

[36]

plat-form in the school room, on the back of which were placed ev-er-green trees. For some scenes a pho-tog-ra-pher's screens were used for a back-ground.

An-na Mor-ris ap-peared af-ter Le-on and Ef-fie. She made a pret-ty pic-ture.

Al-lan Frost, in a clear, pleas-ant voice gave the name of each scene. He was a boy in the Pri-ma-ry class. All liked to hear young Al-lan speak. When he called "The Task," the cur-tain, which had been hung a-cross the plat-form end of the room, was pulled aside, and there sat Ann Green, the lar-gest girl in school look-ing as if she were hard at work at the task of puzz-ling out some prob-lem.

Bes-sie Burns said she would play she was a laun-dress. She did her part well.

The school chil-dren thought up what they would like to be. Hen-ry Hard-ing a dark-eyed, black hair-ed boy said he thought he could get him-self up to look like a pic-ture he seen of an East-ern Grass Sell-er. So he was announced un-der that ti-tle. All thought he looked his part.

It would make too long a sto-ry to tell ev-er-y thing a-bout that show. But the last scene was rath-er an odd one. One far-mer who lived out a short dis-tance from the vil-lage, had an old-fash-ioned ma-chine which had been in his cel-lar for a great man-y years. One of the school boys knew of this queer ar-ti-cle and coaxed the loan of it for the show.

Jer-ry Jar-vis, fath-er of one of the pu-pils, said that he had turned the crank of that ma-chine time and time a-gain when he was a boy, and that he was will-ing to go on the stage with it at that time if it would help a-long the "Show," and raise mon-ey for the "Cause." So when the clos-ing scene came Al-lan Frost called "The Grind-er!"

The folks all en-joyed those Sa-tur-day af-ter-noons. The chil-dren tried to va-ry the shows as much as they could. One day they gave a con-cert. Once they sold home-made can-dy and cakes. Their "Col-o-ni-al Loan" par-ty was much praised. The vil-lage had man-y treas-ures in old chi-na, fur-ni-ture, can-dle sticks, kit-chen ar-ti-cles, pic-tures, guns, swords, and clothes of old times.

All were sur-prised at the ti-dy sum col-lect-ed and man-y a poor ci-ty child re-joiced in the out-ing that mon-ey brought to them through the Fresh Air So-ci-ety.

EGGS IN THE HAY MOW.

"Run out to the barn, An-nie and see if you can find some eggs. I mean to make cake this morn-ing and I shall want four or five," said Mrs. Brown to her lit-tle daugh-ter, An-nie, who had been help-ing her moth-er in the kit-chen work.

Hunt-ing for hen's eggs was great fun for the chil-dren at Brown Farm. Some-times two of them would go out to-geth-er, and each would try to get more eggs than the oth-er, and be the first to reach the kit-chen with a cap or hat full.

An-nie placed a short light lad-der a-gainst a high beam in the barn, climbed up and just as she reached the top, her bright eyes peep-ing in through the hay piled up on the barn-loft floor, she saw a nice hol-low place, some-thing like a small cave, where one wise bid-dy had scratched out a co-sy nest for her-self, and laid some five large eggs. The hen had gone out for a walk or for a lunch-eon, so An-nie

took four of the eggs, put them in-to the crown of her hat, and hast-
ened back to give them to her moth-er.

"May I not beat them up for you, with the whirl-i-gig beat-er, moth-
er, it is so much fun?"

"Yes, you may, An-nie, and it will be quite a help to me."

So on through the morn-ing the lit-tle girl found man-y a use-ful and
plea-sant thing to do. When the work was all done and an out-ing
had been planned for the af-ter-noon, Mrs. Brown said to An-nie,
"This lit-tle verse comes to my mind. I think one of my old-er chil-
dren once learned it at school. It is,

"Work while you work,Play while you play,That is the wayTo be
hap-py and gay.All that you doDo with all your might;Things done
by halvesAre nev-er done right."

THE LOST SKATES.

h, I'll go and see if the ice is firm," said Robin to his friend Marjie, one winter's morning.

He went off carrying his skates, and when he reached the ice he laid them on the bank, and then thought he would have a slide.

Marjie, who had followed Robin to the pond, caught up the skates and went behind a tree and put them on, and was soon skating across the pond. After a while she went to Robin, who was standing by the bank, looking full of dismay.

"Why, Marjie!" he cried, "I never saw you come! I've lost my skates! I left them on the bank and they are gone!"

"Some wicked person must have taken them!" said Marjie.

"I would like to catch him," said Robin.

"Then catch me, Robin!" said Marjie.

Robin gazed at her. Then a light broke over his face.

"Oh, I see!" he cried: "you put them on while I was sliding! Well, now we can take turns with the skates!"

Marjie thought, as she gave Robin a hug, that there was never a dearer friend than he!

NO JOKE AT ALL.

"Ha!" thought Tommy Purr one day,"Here's a chance a joke to play;See him drop upon the floorAll those books, and hear me roar!"

Chuckling to himself in glee,"I do love a joke," said he,Pushed poor Whiskers, just for fun—Down the books came, every one.

But the biggest book of all,Happened on his crown to fall;Tommy roared with might and main,Not with laughter but with pain.

Tommy now has gone to bedWith a big bruise on his head;Vinegar and paper brownCover up his aching crown.

There in sorrow Tommy lies,Wishing he had been more wise;For although those books did fall,His joke proved no joke at all.

WINTER HOLIDAYS.

O it's merry in the winterWhen the holidays come round,When the
air is crisp and frostyAnd the snow is on the ground.

Though Jack Frost may nip your noses,There is nothing that I
knowLike a jolly game of snowballs,Making feet and fingers glow!

You can take your baby sisterFor a voyage in a sleigh;You can build a
monster snow-manThat will pass the time away.

Then there's hanging up the hollyAnd the Christmas
mistletoe,Roasting chestnuts in the firelight,When you can't go out,
you know.

If you try, you can be happyIn a score of different ways.O, it's
wonderful how pleasantAre the winter holidays!

WHEN I GROW UP.

"When I grow up my dress shall beAll made of silk and lace,My hair I'll wear in some fine styleThat best will suit my face;With rings upon my fingers, too,And bracelets on my arms,I'll be the finest lady out,With wondrous mighty charms.

"When I grow up, you understand,I'll always dine at eight,And go to dances and 'At homes,'And sit up very late.I'll never touch rice-puddings then,But pastry eat, and cheese,And always do just what I likeAnd go just where I please.

"When I grow up I'll have no nurse,Nor yet a governess;And lessons will not bother meWhen I grow up, I guess.I'll pay no heed to proper nouns,Nor yet to mood nor tense"—Here nurse put in: "When you grow upLet's hope you'll have some sense!"

THE TEA PARTY.

Little Miss Betty has had a tea-partyEveryone came with an appetite hearty;Animals, dollies, and toys were invited;Bobby was good and our Baby delighted;And when it was over they ran and asked motherIf they might to-morrow have just such another!

TOMMY THE TEASE.

"Here's a pie I found cooling on the bench under the pantry window!" said Tom Sommers. "I'm going to eat it all myself!"

"That is the cook's pie. I saw her making it," said wee George.

"Won't 'ou div me some pie?" asked little Ella.

"No, I won't give you one single bit. This pie is full of plums and juice, I know. Ah! but it will have a good taste! No, Nancy, Susanna, Mariah Anniah you shall not have even a taste of this sweet pie!"

"My name is'nt 'Ria Sannia' 'Ou're a bad boy. 'Ou call me names. 'Ou won't div me any pie! 'Ou eat it all alone!"

"Well, now, this is too bad. Not a knife in any of my pockets! Happen to have a jack-knife with you, Georgie?"

[51]

"No, I haven't any knife."

"What, a big boy like you and no jack-knife?"

"I'd like one, but folks say I'm too little to have one yet. But I'm going to save all my candy money now and buy one for myself."

"Very well, no knife, no pie! It's getting late and I must be going along. It'll take me some time to get there for I must walk slowly so as not to spill a drop of this juicy pie. Good bye."

Saying this, Tom walked away with the pie.

Just then a loud and angry voice was heard shouting, "Where's that pie?" The stout cook came rushing upon the scene, shaking her dish cloth and rolling pin in the air. "Who's got that pie?" she screamed as she ran around and around and back again to the same bench where she had placed the pie to cool. What was her surprise, then, to see the very same pie just where she had left it!

"Oh it's that bad boy, Tom Sommers, who has been playing this trick on me!" she shouted, in a loud voice. "Just let me catch him!"

THE YOUNG LAMB.

One day when brother John came home from market he brought a baby lamb for Maude.

"I thought you'd like this little playmate, sister, you seem to be alone so much. This baby doesn't know how to nibble grass yet and you'll have to get mamma to show you how to bring him up."

Maude was delighted with her present. Her mother took a baby's nurse-bottle and filled it with sweet new milk and in a very short time Lambkin could take, through the rubber tube, all the milk his kind friends would give him.

Maude and her pet made a pretty picture playing together in the meadow.

[53]

Nora, who worked in the kitchen, used to sing an odd little song, some of the words being,

"Little lamb, little lamb,Will you leave your old damAnd sit with me by the nursery fire?You shall have bread and milk,And a cushion of silk,And a cradle as soft as a lamb could desire.

"No! no, little childI'd rather run wildAnd play all the day by the side of my dam;For we love one anotherLike you and your motherAnd she'd cry all the day for the loss of her lamb."

TROTTY'S LESSON.

"Now try to learn this, Trotty. Of course, you're little and don't know much, but when folks ask you how old your brother is you can just say 'a whole hand old!'"

"What for buver?"

"Well, it's because I'm just five years old! You won't have to learn to count yet, but you take a short path and say 'a whole hand old!' Now will you do it?"

"I will try!"

RUTH.

"Company coming to-morrow and not a crumb of cake in the house!" said Mrs. Brown one morning. "Jane's gone and there's all the sweeping to do, the baby to take care of, and three meals a day to get!"

"Mother, mother dear," called Ruth from the next room, "do let me make the cake. I should like nothing better. It would be great fun."

"Great fun! Now that is what one says who knows nothing about it. It would be better to go without any cake at all than to place before our friends some that they cannot eat," replied the tired mother.

"When I was at Aunt Fanny's," said Ruth, "she taught me how to make a kind of cake that we all liked. Uncle John said he could eat all I could make. Do let me try, mother dear."

"Oh, Ruth, what a tease you are. Well, it will keep you quiet for a while and I suppose you must learn somehow."

Then Ruth ran into the kitchen in high glee. First she looked at the fire in the stove as Aunt Fanny had taught her to do. More coal was needed. So she had to go down cellar and bring up as much as she could in the hod. She opened the draughts and put on a little coal at first. When that had kindled she put on a little more. She took a whisk and swept out the stove oven. Then she put more water into the kettle on on top of the stove. Soon it was time to close the draughts. She put her hand into the oven to feel how hot it was just as she had seen her Aunt Fanny do.

When the stove was as she wanted it, Ruth ran out to the barn and found four warm eggs in nests among the hay. These she brought into the house, and breaking them into a bowl, began to beat them up quickly. Next she took a yellow dish from the dresser and put into it one cup of butter and two cups of sugar. For a long time she mixed these two together until they were "all one," as she called it.

Next she put the four beaten eggs into the bowl with the butter and sugar, and beat them until her little hands ached. Then she measured out three cups of flour and sifted it into another dish. With this she put two teaspoonfuls of baking powder, and then sifted flour and baking powder together. After this was done, she added a little of it at a time to the mixture of butter and eggs, beating away until all the flour had been used up. Then she put into it a teaspoonful of vanilla essence and added enough milk to make

[57]

a thick batter. Little pans shaped like hearts and rounds, and one large round pan were then well greased, and the beaten up cake put into each pan until it was half full. Then the pans of cake were set into the oven and in ten or fifteen minutes all the tiny "hearts and rounds" were baked a light brown, while the large pan had to stay baking ten or fifteen minutes more.

A very happy child was young Ruth when she took out her pans of cake.

Her father, mother, brothers and the "company" who arrived the next day thought it the "nicest cake ever made by so young a little girl."

MISCHIEVOUS BABY.

Full of mischief? Well, yes, may be,Else he would not be a baby.But—when he's asleep, dear me,What baby could more quiet be?

End of the book.

www.ingramcontent.com/pod-product-compliance
Lightning Source LLC
Chambersburg PA
CBHW060004300526
45794CB00003B/1073